,b 15321113

You and Your Environment

A DISCOVERY SCIENCE Primary Grades Unit

S0-FAE-050

HAM
HT
151
Y68
1998

Elizabeth A. Sherwood

Robert A. Williams

David A. Winnett

Robert E. Rockwell

Dale Seymour Publications®

Faculty of Education I.R.C.
MAR 23 1999
Brock University

WITHDRAWN

Contributing authors: *Lori Burns, Lela DeToye, Barbara Goldenhersh, Ann Scates, Gale Thacker, Kathy Weber, Sharon Winnett, Cathy Wright*

Field-test sites: *Edwardsville, Illinois Community School; Hillsboro, Illinois Community School*

This book is published by Dale Seymour Publications®, an imprint of Addison Wesley Longman, Inc.

Dale Seymour Publications
10 Bank Street
White Plains, New York 10602
Customer Service: 800-872-1100

Managing Editor: *Catherine Anderson*
Project Editor: *Mali Apple*
Production/Manufacturing Director: *Janet Yearian*
Senior Production Coordinator: *Fiona Santoianni*
Design Director: *Phyllis Aycock*
Cover and Text Design: *Christy Butterfield*
Cover Illustration: *Ed Taber*
Classroom Photographs: *Bill Brinson*
Composition: *Claire Flaherty*
Illustrations: *Teresa Dillon*

The blackline masters in this publication are designed to be used with appropriate duplicating equipment to reproduce copies for classroom use. Addison Wesley Publishing Company grants permission to classroom teachers to reproduce these masters.

Copyright © 1998 by Addison Wesley Publishing Company. Printed in the United States of America.

This Book Is Printed
on Recycled Paper

Order number 36841
ISBN 0-201-49663-1

1 2 3 4 5 6 7 8 9 10 - ML - 01 00 99 98 97

CONTENTS

Introduction

The environment is possibly the single most important science topic to which we introduce children. All of our scientific knowledge is for nothing if we cannot protect and maintain the environment in which we all live. This unit exposes children to a variety of environmental issues and encourages them to make meaningful assessments of what they observe and experience.

As in all the Discovery Science units, the child is at the center of the exploration and determines the direction in which the investigation will progress. What should your students discover about their environment—what it consists of and what affects it—as they engage in the activities in this unit?

Science Concepts

Three main science concepts will be addressed in this unit:

1. Everything around us is part of our environment.

2. We can observe and cause changes in our environment.

3. We can help take care of our environment.

Everything around us is part of our environment. Our environment is all that surrounds us: the air we breath, the soil we stand on and grow our food in, the structures we build to house our possessions and ourselves. It encompasses both the components of the natural world and the products of society. You will find it challenging and rewarding to help young investigators explore the many facets of the word *environment*. It is also important for children to develop an understanding that changes in the natural or manufactured elements of our environment directly affect all other aspects of the environment. Every environmental element plays a role in the maintenance of a quality of life that will allow future generations to live in a healthy, well-cared-for world.

We can observe and cause changes in our environment. We learn about our environment through careful observation with all of our senses. We must observe and monitor the state of our environment to be aware of changes that occur. This ongoing observation allows us to focus on the overall impact that society is having on environmental quality. And, with such information, we can become knowledgeable advocates for and participants in caring for the environment.

We can help take care of our environment. Taking care of the environment is everyone's responsibility. Young and old should share in the stewardship of the air we breath and the water we drink. We can nurture in children a desire and commitment to do their part in preserving the natural beauty of their surroundings and the health of the planet Earth.

The activities in this unit are organized to allow continuous development of the science concepts being studied and function best if used in the order presented.

Getting Ready

To complete many of the activities in this unit, you will need to add the following materials to the Discovery Center:

- A collection of natural objects, such as soil samples, clean sand, sticks, twigs, and rocks

- A collection of manufactured objects, such as small plastic bags, pencils, plastic straws, plastic insects, pieces of concrete, bricks, and artificial flowers

- A variety of tools to enhance the children's observations, such as magnifiers, magnets, picture identification books, containers for sorting objects, funnels, rulers, thermometers, microscopes, pH and cobalt chloride paper, and eyedroppers

- Printed material—reference books, newspaper articles, magazine articles—related to the topics of environmental science, including such areas as pollution, recycling, and plant and animal classification

You will also need chart paper and colored markers on hand for creating Discovery Charts.

Free Discovery

Free Discovery is an opportunity for the children to talk about what they already know or believe about the environment and to become acquainted with some of the materials they will be working with in the *You and Your Environment* unit.

Free Discovery is observation, exploration, and interaction that proceeds at the children's own pace, a means to support their curiosity about the world around them. It offers them the freedom to explore in a nonthreatening environment, eliminating the fear of getting "wrong" answers. As the children are in control of their actions, the process builds their self-esteem. In this secure and comfortable environment, children are able to fulfill their natural eagerness to search for solutions to their own questions of *why, what, how,* and *when*—in their own way.

During this free exploration, the children experience the materials as learning resources. The time they spend investigating on their own may well be some of their most productive and constructive learning time.

Exploratory freedom reigns in Free Discovery, and it can be a difficult time for adults. We are often tempted to step in at this learning phase, intercepting children's natural curiosity with questions and challenges that are adult-initiated rather than child-initiated. Children are often unprepared for such interruption. We must remind ourselves that Free Discovery is a time for children to explore the materials in their own way.

Conducting the Free Discovery Session

Before starting the first activity, create a class Discovery Chart of what the children already know about their environment. Talk with them about the elements of the environment that they will be exploring. Ask such questions as, "What do you think the word *environment* means? What things are part of your environment? What things are not part of your environment?"

Challenge the children to think of as many words as they can to describe what is found in their environment. As they share their ideas, consider whether any of their questions about the environment can be incorporated into the activities that will follow.

Keep the chart posted in the room throughout the unit, and from time to time ask the children if they would like to add to it or to change any of the information it contains.

Supply the children with hand lenses and magnifiers, and take them outside to explore. While outside, have the children record their findings in their Discovery Journals. When the class returns indoors, they can compare their individual discoveries to the ideas listed on the class Discovery Chart and add or adjust information as appropriate. This process will help the children structure their understanding as well as assist in placing isolated pieces of information into a meaningful context.

Introduce the children to the materials that will be used in the activities, including the sets of natural and manufactured objects that you have added to the Discovery Center. If any materials require special care, talk about them with the children.

During Free Discovery, talk informally with the children about their explorations. Ask questions to assess what they are doing and thinking about as they work. Monitor them to be sure investigations are being done safely. The children may come to these initial activities with useful observations they have already made on their own. Encourage them to record any interesting observations in their Discovery Journals.

You may want to use this opportunity to apply the Success in Science Inventory (see page 23) to evaluate the children's interest and involvement in science. An informal, direct observation of the manner in which the children approach the challenge of scientific investigation will reveal useful information that you can apply later in your interactions with them.

Additional Resources

You may want to add some of these books to the Discovery Center:

- *Walk in the Desert* by Caroline Arnold (Englewood Cliffs, N.J.: Silver Burdett Press, 1990) introduces children to plants and animals that live in the desert.

- *Walk in the Woods* by Caroline Arnold (Englewood Cliffs, N.J.: Silver Burdett Press, 1990) describes some of the plants and animals that live in the forest and investigates how the forest changes with each new season.

- *Walk up a Mountain* by Caroline Arnold (Englewood Cliffs, N.J.: Silver Burdett Press, 1990) describes the geographic features of mountains (and how to climb them!) and introduces plants and animals that live there.

- *What Can We Do About . . . ?* by Donna Bailey (New York: Franklin Watts, 1991–1992) is a series of books that looks at today's most pressing environmental issues and explores ways in which individuals, families, and local groups can have a positive impact. Each book—*What Can We Do About Litter? Noise and Fumes? Recycling Garbage? Wasting Water? Conserving Energy?* and *Protecting Nature?*—talks about the main causes and the possible solutions of a particular issue.

- *Pollution* by Herta S. Breiter (Milwaukee: Raintree Steck-Vaughn Books, 1987) offers a clear overview of the subject.

- *The World About Us* by Michael Bright (New York: Franklin Watts, 1991) is an important series that introduces young people to today's most complex environmental problems and what needs to be done to preserve our world. The titles in this series are *Acid Rain, Tropical Rainforest, The Greenhouse Effect,* and *The Ozone Layer.*

- *Up North at the Cabin* by Martha W. Chall (New York: Lothrop, Lee and Shepard Books, 1992) explores memories of family trips including water activities such as swimming, canoeing, and water-skiing.

- *The Magic School Bus at the Waterworks* by Joanna Cole (New York: Scholastic, 1993) explores the question of how the water cycle supplies people with water.

- *In the Small, Small Pond* by Denise Fleming (New York: Henry Holt and Company, 1993) uses simple rhyming verse to introduce children to life in a pond.

- *Box Turtle at Long Pond* by William T. George (New York: Greenwillow Books, 1989) is a story told from a turtle's point of view as he tries to meet his basic needs of water, food, shelter, and safety from predators.

- *Caring for Our Air* by Carol Greene (Hillside, N.J.: Enslow Publishers, 1991) recommends practical steps to curb air pollution.

- *Recycling* by Tony Hare (New York: Franklin Watts, 1991) explains why recycling is important, how it is done, and what people gain by it.

- *Amy Loves the Rain* by Julia Hoban (New York: HarperCollins Children's Books, 1989) offers young children the opportunity to become more aware of the sounds and colors of a rainy day.

- *Earthwise at Home: A Guide to the Care and Feeding of Your Planet* by Linda Lowery (Minneapolis: Lerner Group, 1992) is an excellent tool to help people recycle, reuse, and preserve materials at home.

- *Wump World* by Bill Peet (Boston: Houghton Mifflin, 1991) is a delightfully illustrated tale of peace-loving, grass-eating creatures whose world is ruined by pollution and the misuse of natural resources.

- *Conservation and Pollution* by Laurence Santrey (Mahwah, N.J.: Troll Communications, 1985) explains how the growth of industry in modern times has brought about the pollution of air, water, and land as well as the depletion of natural resources, and emphasizes the importance of conservation.

- *Here Comes the Recycling Truck!* by Meyer Seltzer (Morton Grove, Ill.: Albert Whitman and Company, 1992) follows a garbage truck not to the dump, but to the recycling center.

- *Air Pollution* by Darlene Stille (Danbury, Ct.: Children's Press, 1990) presents scientific facts about air pollution.

- *The Greenhouse Effect* by Darlene Stille (Danbury, Ct.: Children's Press, 1990) explains what a greenhouse is, how it relates to global warming, and how we can stop the greenhouse effect.

- *Different Kinds of Plants* by Colin Walker (Cleveland: Modern Curriculum Press, 1988) describes plant characteristics and how they determine the way plants are classified into groups or families.

- *Weather on Earth* by Colin Walker (Cleveland: Modern Curriculum Press, 1989) explains common weather patterns and phenomena that are used in forecasting.

- *Trash!* by Charlotte Wilcox (Minneapolis: Lerner Group, 1989) explores what happens to garbage after it is collected.

Discovery Science

The Discovery Science program is designed to expose children to much more than science skills and concepts. It gives children the opportunity to explore, experiment, create, and problem solve. It encourages them to refine their use of language as they talk about what they are doing or explain what they have discovered. It allows them to apply their emerging mathematical skills in the meaningful context of exploration. And it provides teachers with a curricular framework that capitalizes on the spirit of excitement for discovery that dwells in the minds of children, young and old.

Children come to the educational setting with diverse backgrounds and experiences. Discovery Science integrates science, mathematics, and literacy in a curriculum that recognizes and builds from this diversity.

Using the Discovery Science Units

Traditional primary grades science programs often try to cover a great deal of information in the short school year. The Discovery Science units for the primary grades explore fewer topics in much greater depth.

Plan on spending about eight to ten weeks on each unit. The time required for each activity depends on how much classroom time the teacher wants to devote to science. There is enough material in each activity—including the Additional Stimulation ideas (which include art, literature, and social studies extensions)—for about a week's worth of exploration, or three to four sessions. At a minimum, each activity will require about an hour, including preparation time.

The flexibility of the Discovery Science program allows you to take one of two approaches to using the units in your science program. You can build your science curriculum around Discovery Science units. The set of four units recommended at each grade level stands alone as a complete science curriculum and represents the domains generally considered important for the primary grades: physical, life, and environmental science. We suggest that you select the four units recommended for your grade level, unless your district has other requirements for the sequence of topics in your science program. For grade 1, the recommended units are *The Mysteries of Light* (physical science),

The Wonders of Water (physical science), *You and Your Environment* (environmental science), and *Animals and Their Homes* (life science).

Alternatively, you may choose to supplement or enhance your existing curriculum with a favorite unit or two. Units may be used at one grade higher or lower than the designated level.

Teaching Discovery Science

Discovery Science visualizes children as learners actively constructing knowledge rather than passively taking in information. Through their activity, children form knowledge and make it their own.

GOALS FOR PRIMARY GRADES SCIENCE

1. To provide an environment that supports active discovery.

2. To promote the development of fundamental problem-solving skills.

3. To promote personality dispositions indicative of good scientific problem solvers.

4. To promote children's awareness of careers in science, mathematics, and technology.

5. To raise children's comfort and confidence level with science through conscious efforts to counter bias against science.

6. To promote development of a knowledge base of basic scientific principles and laws, the foundation upon which a clear and accurate understanding of the world can develop. A solid foundation reduces the risk of children acquiring misconceptions that may hinder their understanding of more complex science concepts later.

The inquiry model that prevails in Discovery Science begins with asking the children: *What do you know about this topic?* This is followed by Free Discovery, in which the children explore the new materials on their own. Then, they are asked: *What did you learn?* This question is followed by experiences designed to encourage the children to ask questions and to seek their own answers. Through this process, children are *empowered* to become scientists.

To be effective, a science program must emphasize interaction with the environment, natural as well as social. To promote social interaction, the teacher and the children in Discovery Science have specific roles.

THE ROLE OF THE TEACHER

- To encourage children to explore and experiment independently
- To create an atmosphere conducive to learning
- To introduce new ideas, materials, and procedures
- To encourage inquiry and creativity
- To model inquiry, questioning, and problem solving
- To model safe practices
- To provide sufficient materials, information, and space
- To support developmentally appropriate activity
- To assess and evaluate children's learning

THE ROLE OF THE CHILDREN

- To care for and function independently
- To understand that they are in control of their actions
- To feel good about discovery
- To cooperate with other children
- To collect data and document activities
- To explore materials and ideas
- To realize that answers are not right or wrong but simply the result of inquiry
- To communicate their experiences

Discovery Groups

We encourage teachers to have children work in small groups whenever the nature of the activity allows for this type of inter-action. We refer to these heterogeneous, collaborative groups as Discovery Groups to reinforce the importance of inquiry and investigation. In some activities, it will be appropriate to assign each child a role within the group, such as Principal Investigator (directs the investigation), Lab Manager (gathers materials and cleans up), Recorder (keeps track of what is discovered), and Reporter (shares the group's findings with the class).

When children work in interactive groups, several exciting things happen. The investigation is enhanced, in that now there are several inquiring minds generating questions and trying to understand the observed phenomena. The skills of observation, classification, and communication take on new importance, as they become the vehicles by which the group travels together in the directions the inquiry takes them. Management of the children and equipment becomes easier, as the teacher has only to deal with several groups rather than many individuals.

Limiting the Number of Concepts Explored

Each unit in the Discovery Science program addresses a relatively few number of science concepts.

Textbooks are often packed full of concepts and terms that children are expected to absorb during the brief school year. For most young learners, this is far too much in too little time. A hurried exposure to science may fail to provide the opportunity for the rich conceptual development that is possible with a more coherent, thoughtful approach that supports quality over quantity. When learning is centered around a small number of core concepts, the learner can spend enough time with the materials and concepts to master them.

Too often, instead of giving children the self-confidence that comes with mastering new ideas or skills, we move them quickly from one topic to the next. We are subtly teaching them to be satisfied with incompetence. With a limited number of topics, children have more opportunities to experience feelings of competence and mastery.

Repetition will reinforce children's awareness of their own competence and the confidence that awareness brings. Materials should be accessible and the curriculum developed in such a way that children can return to or repeat experiences that they may have completed some time ago.

Supporting Emerging Language and Literacy Skills

The Discovery Science program is designed to familiarize children with the process of asking a question and looking for an answer, and it encourages children to devise their own ways to communicate their experiences. As children seek to describe their observations accurately and to share their discoveries, they will improve their use of language and expand their vocabulary. Alternative methods of communication—such as drawings, charts, and graphs—are introduced and used. The language focus should remain on effective communication and interesting and accurate content rather than precise spelling, grammar, and penmanship.

Group experiences model diverse uses of language and literacy and encourage sharing and collaboration, which require meaningful oral and written communication.

Discovery Charts

Discovery Charts, lists of "what we know," are used periodically to record what children know and to give direction to class planning. They communicate to children in a concrete way that what they are doing is important enough to write down and remember. The first Discovery Chart is created at the start of the unit, during Free Discovery, to assess children's current level of understanding. Variations on the basic Discovery Chart are suggested throughout the activities.

Make additions to Discovery Charts whenever significant new information is generated. You may want to add new concepts in a different color. This will help emphasize to children, and to families who see the Discovery Charts on the wall, that more knowledge is being acquired.

Review the Discovery Charts with children often to reinforce the science concepts and to support emerging literacy skills. At times, children may realize that a statement written earlier is inaccurate. For example, an early Discovery Chart may state that "magnets pick up metal," yet the children have since discovered that there are some kinds of metal that magnets will not attract. When children become aware of the discrepancy between an earlier statement and their current knowledge, help them to create a new, more accurate statement.

You may want to revisit the charts with the class later in the year, long after work on a unit is complete, to convey the value and consistency of the information the children have acquired.

Discovery Journals

Discovery Journals are a key component of Discovery Science. They document the children's explorations, serve as a means of communicating to others, and support emerging literacy skills. It is a rewarding experience for children to look back at their entries and see their own progress. The journals are also a permanent record of what the children have learned that they can share with their families.

The children will need a separate Discovery Journal for each unit. An inexpensive three-ring plastic binder is ideal and will last all year. The cover can be labeled *Discovery Science* with a permanent marker, and the children can make title pages for each unit. The binder allows flexibility as the children create their journals, as they can insert drawings and extra pages as needed. When the unit is complete, the pages can be removed and stapled or bound together to form a Discovery Journal for the unit. As an alternative to binders, Discovery Journals may be preassembled, allowing at least one sheet of paper per activity, and stapled together. Children can make and decorate construction-paper covers.

Blackline masters are provided for some of the activities. Use these Discovery Pages whenever you like to supplement the children's Discovery Journal entries or simply to provide one model for how their responses to an activity might be recorded. Keep in mind that other recording methods are always appropriate.

The page of clip art at the back of the book will inspire and help you and your students prepare your own charts and tables. Children may want to affix some of the images to pages of their Discovery Journals to illustrate what they have done and learned.

Making Connections to Other Areas

The activities and associated extension ideas in each unit present many opportunities to connect the science experiences with mathematics, technology, art, and other areas. In addition, several take-home activities are offered as a way to involve the family in what the child is learning at school.

Connections to Mathematics

Measurement and basic arithmetic skills are needed to quantify observations. Science discovery and investigation provide the perfect opportunity for children to apply graphing, charting, and data-analysis skills to real problem-solving situations.

More important, when mathematics is integrated into the science curriculum, children learn science and mathematics skills together as part of a unified curriculum. Showing children the connection of numbers to the practical examples from science enables them to begin to operationalize mathematical skills.

Connections to Language

Discovery Science offers continuous opportunities for written and oral language development. Children are encouraged to share their ideas with the class as Discovery Charts are generated and in their small Discovery Groups as they work through activities. Discovery Journals support clear written communication about observations and speculations.

The Science Vocabulary in each activity is the specialized vocabulary that children must comprehend to fully understand the science concepts they are exploring. We encourage you to work with the children to develop operational definitions of the words that are introduced. The *operational definition* of a word is simply the meaning the children derive that fits with their own ongoing exploration of the concept. We are trying to give children the confidence to explore and discover on their own—to have power over the direction their inquiry follows. Encouraging them to use their own operational definitions will allow them to use language more freely. Misconceptions of word meanings are best resolved through additional experience rather than verbal correction of their understanding.

Connections to the Family

As the child's first caregiver and teacher, parents have both the right and the responsibility to be involved in their child's formal education. Research conducted in a variety of educational settings over the past three decades suggests that parents who establish a learning environment in the home, who stimulate their children's interest in learning, and who support their children's natural curiosity, foster attitudes that help ensure their children's academic achievement. In addition, involved parents develop more positive attitudes toward the school and its goals. (R. E. Rockwell, L. C. Andre, and M. K. Hawley, *Parents and Teachers as Partners: Issues and Challenges.* Fort Worth, Texas: Harcourt Brace College Publishers, 1996)

Families and educators have a common goal: concern for the children. Home and school are both important functional areas for children. Mutual respect and support between home and school is essential for helping children to develop and learn and for creating the most effective learning environment. Early childhood and primary grades programs can encourage parents to be part of the education process. The Discovery Science program provides a natural avenue for children, families, and teachers to work together.

THE ROLE OF THE FAMILY

- To encourage the child's own discovery process
- To model inquiry and problem solving
- To resist answering and solving discovery activities before the child has done so
- To enjoy doing science activities with the child
- To feel free to communicate with the child's teacher, to ask questions, and to seek additional information when needed
- To listen to and give information to the child, and to remember that it is all right for any participant to make mistakes or to say "I don't know"

- To share available resources from home, such as junk materials for making things or information and materials related to occupations or hobbies that correspond to the unit topic

Family activities reinforce what the children are learning at school. They empower children by giving them the opportunity to share their knowledge with their families. Each family activity idea is presented in a note that you send home with the children. You may want children to record what they learn at home in their Discovery Journals for sharing with the class later.

Developing Science Process Skills

The success of the Discovery Science approach to learning science will be evident in the children's ability to perform the skills of inquiry, more generally called *science process skills*. Most approaches to encouraging the development of science process skills are aimed at learners who have reached a level of mental development that allows them to reason and understand abstract ideas.

This curriculum takes a *developmental approach* to teaching young children the skills of research and investigation, beginning with the premise that young learners require focus and guidance in the initial steps of acquiring these skills. The Discovery Science program presents the skills in a way that assists young learners in their early efforts with the specific processes.

Activities for this unit have been designed to facilitate this process. For example, if we want children to use their senses to observe certain physical characteristics of the objects they are investigating, we select activities that highlight the desired observations, thus helping them to focus their senses on the relevant observations. More sophisticated science process skills developed in the unit are making inferences and making predictions. Again, specific activities have been developed to provide the teacher with ideal conditions in which to guide the children to making their own inferences and predictions.

Following are descriptions of the science process skills developed in this unit.

Focused Observation

Focused Observation activities allow teacher-directed quality control over the types of observations the children are making. Children are recording these observations in their minds. Later, they can recall an observation and fit it into a larger conceptual framework that allows them to make sense of what they are doing or learning.

Because children will use current observations as a basis on which to build future understanding, you have two major instructional concerns. First, there are observations about each science theme that children need to make; if they are not made, the children will not begin to understand the concepts. Second, children are continually making inferences about what they have observed. Some of these inferences are correct, and some may not be.

Focused Observation activities are designed to direct children's observations to specific aspects of each concept. You will frequently ask the children to organize their observations and to make them more precise. The children will be asked to isolate various factors that affect their subject and to alter them to make new observations regarding the effect these changes have. For example, if the children are rolling a ball down an inclined plane, they may be asked what would happen if they changed the angle of the plane.

Observing to Classify

Encouraging children to make use of their observations reinforces the importance of being a good observer. Classification tasks provide children with an opportunity to make decisions and to be in control. A successfully organized group of objects gives them immediate satisfaction in knowing that the task is over and has been done well—similar to the feeling adults experience when all the pieces of a puzzle fit together.

Organizing and Communicating Observations

Science seeks to find order and structure in our world. Free Discovery, Focused Observation, and Observing to Classify are the initial experiences children need if they are to begin establishing order in their world. Your next task is to encourage them to make meaningful drawings in their Discovery Journals and to create charts and graphs to help them describe their observations. Through this process, they will begin to understand the need for orderly record keeping and systematic analysis of information— as well as the importance of clear communication—at their level, of course. In addition, they will see that much of what they are learning about numbers and simple arithmetic is quite useful in scientific discovery.

Guided Inference

When we make inferences, we are attempting to explain what we have observed. Young learners need guidance to develop this skill; they are still operating at a concrete level of thinking and must be encouraged to explain their thoughts. Moreover, their frame of reference is limited since they have not yet compiled a broad base of knowledge and understanding.

You can guide children in their initial attempts at formulating inferences by setting the stage and coordinating the actors. When you direct children to attempt activities that allow them to observe interesting yet familiar phenomena, and then to explain in their own words why something behaved the way it did, you are guiding their inferences.

Guided Prediction

After experimenting with certain materials, children will be asked to predict how other materials will respond to the same conditions. Your attempts to guide their predictions should begin with simple forecasts of events that have yet to take place. You must make sure their initial predictions are directly related to the frames of reference they have developed during the course of the discovery activity.

Encouraging Family Involvement

In addition to sending home and reviewing the suggested family activities, there are many other steps you can take to involve families in their children's learning experience.

Introducing Discovery Science: A Family Meeting

Invite families to be a part of a Discovery Science hands-on meeting. In the meeting, you will talk with them about the program and how it will be implemented. The major focus of the meeting is to inform families of the emphasis that the Discovery Science curriculum places upon working with parents as partners in the education of their children.

Prepare the Discovery Center to allow families to interact with some of the Discovery Science activities and materials in the same way their children will. Introduce the activities that you will periodically be sending home. During the meeting, you may discover special interests or related skills some family members have and would be willing to share with the class.

After attending the meeting, families will be more adept at supporting, modeling, and discussing Discovery Science with their children.

Discovery Science Newsletter

Create a Discovery Science newsletter, either as a separate piece or as a portion of a general newsletter. In the newsletter, inform families of science-related activities at school and in the community, including field trips, classroom visitors, and great discoveries that will help keep interest and input coming.

Family Letters and Discovery Science Notes

Send a letter home to families at the start of each Discovery Science unit to introduce the topic and to ask for support and ideas for resources. You might mention that the children will periodically be bringing home activities to share with their families, and that any observations or comments families have to offer on these experiences would be quite welcome.

Send home brief notes to update families on current activities, to remind them of an upcoming field trip or event, or to relate their child's recent discovery.

Family Volunteers

Discovery Science can provide opportunities and access for families to get involved, from offering resources and materials to volunteering at the school. Family volunteers can enrich the learning process and expand the learning environment for children as they share their skills, personal expertise, and the enthusiasm of discovery.

The Discovery Center

A well-organized and well-maintained science center offers a central focus for a successful science program. The Discovery Center sets the stage for exploration. It provides ample materials in an accessible way, has safe and orderly workspaces, and serves as a resource and library. The Discovery Center also serves as the storage site for materials to be used elsewhere.

By its very nature, the Discovery Center promotes problem solving and positive risk taking because children work largely on their own. Children learn to make independent decisions as they explore concepts designed to teach the how-to of science rather than words and facts.

The size and organization of your classroom will determine your Discovery Center's total area. When designing your center, consider how many children you would like it to accommodate at one time.

Collecting Materials for the Discovery Center

Materials in the Discovery Center should be sturdy, simple, and easy to handle. If space does not allow for a permanent center, select materials that can be set up quickly and stored easily.

The Discovery Center should contain the following basic equipment:

- safety goggles
- laboratory coats (paint aprons or smocks)
- magnifying devices such as hand lenses, bug boxes, and two-way magnifiers
- double-pan balance with standard and nonstandard units of mass
- standard and nonstandard measuring devices for length and volume
- spoons, scoops, droppers, and forceps
- containers such as bowls, bottles, and cups
- sorting and storage containers such as egg cartons and clear plastic vials with lids
- cardboard or plastic foam food-packaging trays for sorting and mess containment

- writing materials
- cleanup equipment such as buckets, sponges, dustpans, and hand brooms

Setting Up the Discovery Center

Storage space must be thoughtfully designed to meet your classroom's instructional needs. Several types of storage are necessary.

The materials listed above should be out and available at all times, promoting their use and encouraging children to find new functions for them. Shelves, tables, and pegboard are useful for this type of storage.

Some materials must be stored out of the way until needed. Plastic storage tubs are an excellent choice: they come in a variety of sizes and stack easily, allowing whole sets of materials to be stored together. The availability of clear lids and a variety of colors increases their flexibility. They can be made accessible to the children or stored out of reach.

Other materials must be available but not necessarily out on shelves. Resealable plastic bags are useful for containing small sets of materials. Small tubs, boxes, and crates are also helpful.

All storage space and containers should be easy to clean and label, inexpensive, and easy for children to use and keep in order. Racks, hooks, shelves, and storage closets should be labeled.

Also consider the following when designing your Discovery Center:

- Clutter-free surfaces for work areas.
- Places on shelves, tables, or the floor to leave materials for an extended time or study.
- Areas should be easy to clean and cleanup materials readily available. Responsibility for accidents, along with normal messes, is part of science training.
- Water should be available either from a sink or special containers. Water in the area means less traffic to the taps in the bathrooms.

Share special care or storage requirements with the children when you introduce them to new materials. Discuss safety rules each time a new material or piece of equipment is added to the Discovery Center. Model safe behavior, and set clear limits to enable children to handle and interact with the materials safely.

Assessment

The assessment and evaluation procedures used in Discovery Science are consistent with sound test and measurement approaches. They have been developed to be practical and informative for the primary classroom setting.

Assessment and evaluation in Discovery Science are closely tied to instruction and are embedded in the learning cycle rather than being "tacked on," as a caboose at the end of the train. Several train engines are spread throughout the line of cars—engines that give power and purpose to the learning activities. When assessment measures are inseparable from the curriculum and the instructional approach, we say they are *authentic*. Discovery Science uses authentic assessment measures in such a way that both teachers and children perceive the assessment as an extension of the learning process.

Be aware of the diversity of the developmental levels of children in your classroom. Nothing in your evaluation should discourage children in the growth of their inquiry skills or, even worse, set their present attitude against scientific inquiry—an attitude they may well possess the rest of their lives. A willingness to think, to explore, and to search for answers is critical for the development of good problem-solving skills.

The assessment system used in Discovery Science has three components: the Success in Science Inventory, curriculum-embedded assessment, and the use of Discovery Charts.

Using the Success in Science Inventory

The Success in Science Inventory (SSI) is a checklist used to record children's dispositions toward scientific inquiry. When certain behaviors or choices are made by a child, we begin to formulate an understanding of the level of interest and enthusiasm that child has for discovery.

Although the SSI may be used at any time in the curriculum, we recommend that it be used during each unit's Free Discovery period to assess the children's interaction with materials in the center and with each other. Evaluate each child in each of the four science dispositions throughout the year. The suggested levels of performance are Not Apparent, Emerging, and Developed. To simplify scoring, scale of 1 to 3 is suggested.

Evaluation using the SSI will give you a picture of how the class is progressing overall. You will know that Free Discovery is successful when these early problem-solving behaviors emerge in the children. As you observe their behavior, you will get a feel for when it is time to move on to the next phase of Discovery Science. The children will show that they are ready to do more.

To use the SSI, administer it during the Free Discovery session. You may elect to observe and record dispositions for all children each time or to select certain children at different times. Observe and record children's behavior for each of the four science dispositions, indicating the child's level within a particular disposition. The more marks a child receives, the greater the indication of success in science.

The SSI assesses four science dispositions:

1. The child manipulates objects for useful observations. *Does the child explore new materials placed in the Discovery Center in a thoughtful way?*

2. The child seeks a clear understanding of the questions *who, what, where,* and *when*—the facts. *When observing something unique on a field trip, does the child ask relevant questions?*

3. The child seeks reasons: asks the question *why* and tries to answer it through further exploration. *As the child works on a project that continues to fail, does the child persist in trying alternatives?*

4. The child communicates the results of observations and investigations. *Does the child talk with you or others about Discovery Science activities?*

Using Curriculum-Embedded Assessment

The second assessment instrument used in Discovery Science is curriculum-embedded assessment, which is in several forms.

Assessing the Activity

Assessing the Activity is found at the end of each activity. It is a formative evaluation that provides ongoing information about how successfully the children are mastering skills and understanding concepts. If the children are unable to meet the expectations of the task, you can act immediately to guide them toward better understanding of the concepts. You may want to keep a record of these formative evaluations for each child in individual portfolios.

Success in Science Inventory

**Science
Dispositions**

Child's Name	1	2	3	4	Comments

1. Manipulates objects for useful observations.

2. Seeks a clear understanding of the questions *who, what, where,* and *when*—the facts.

3. Seeks reason. Asks the question *why* and tries to answer it through further explorations.

4. Communicates the results of observations and investigations.

Checkpoint Activity

The Checkpoint Activity at the end of the unit is a summative look at how well children have developed the desired skills. Although not to be considered a final unit test, the Checkpoint Activity does provide an opportunity for you to observe the children's level of skill mastery. If children have performed well on the Assessing the Activities, they should have little trouble completing the Checkpoint Activity.

Additional Stimulation Activities

The Additional Stimulation ideas suggested in each activity will assist you in expanding the children's newly acquired knowledge and incorporating it into other curricular areas. These mini-activities can also serve to reinforce a science concept when the children have not completely mastered it during the main activity.

Discovery Journals

The single most important thing to remember when you review the children's Discovery Journals is that *they belong to the children*. They are the children's own record of their learning and discovery. Letter grades, happy or sad faces, or comments written on their pages will quickly eliminate the children's spontaneity, their sense of ownership, and the pride and improvement in skill that comes from *self*-assessment.

Using Discovery Charts

When created by the class at the beginning of a unit, Discovery Charts serve as a preassessment. They tell you what the children as a whole already know, and they can make you aware of misconceptions.

When you take the time to refer to an old chart, add to it, or create a new one, the children will see that they are learning. Discovery Charts also can be used as a part of individual assessment, as they contain the main body of knowledge generated by the children themselves. Each child should have an understanding of most if not all of the information the Discovery Charts contain.

Surveying the School Yard

Children have a limited awareness of the enormous reservoir of living things that surrounds them. In this series of activities, they will begin to discover the incredible variety and quantity of the living things—plants and animals—and manufactured objects in their immediate environment. With a little help from you, they will be awed by the diversity of plants and animals in our world.

CONNECTIONS

TO LANGUAGE

Written Language—The children create lists of the natural and manufactured items they find in the school yard.

TO THE FAMILY

This activity gives children an opportunity to share with their families what they are discovering about their environment. Send a note home with the children explaining the survey the children conducted at school. Families can assist the children with completing a survey of their own backyards or other environments.

Your child has been learning about the fantastic abundance and variety of natural and manufactured things in our environment. This week we did a school-yard survey. We discovered living and nonliving things like worms, birds, flowers, grass, paper, aluminum cans, plastic, and glass. As an extension of this activity, we would like you and your child to do a survey in your own backyard or neighborhood. Take a pencil and paper on your walk, and list the items you find in these two categories:

    Natural Objects   Manufactured Objects

Talk with your child about how to classify each item you find. Send the lists you make to school with your child.

Before the Activity

Collect clipboards, or make writing platforms from cardboard and binder clips.

Science Process Skill

Focused Observation

Science Concept

Everything around us is part of our environment.

Science Vocabulary

environment

identify

manufactured

organism

plant and animal names

survey

Materials

picture-identification books *(for helping identify what the children find)*

clipboards

map-making or model-making materials *(for creating a map or model of the school yard)*

"What's in Our Environment?" Discovery Page *(optional; see page 83)*

What to Do

1. Talk with the children about the plants, animals, and other elements of nature that they know are present in the school yard. Also ask about the manufactured things that are found in the school yard.

   Make two Discovery Charts listing the natural and manufactured objects the children expect to find when they explore the school yard. You may have to remind them that insects and worms are animals, that paper and swing sets are both examples of manufactured materials, and that seeds and flowers are parts of plants.

2. Give each Discovery Group a clipboard, and take the children outside to explore their environment. Ask them to draw or list all the natural and manufactured things they see, along with the location where they saw them. The lists might include squirrels, playground equipment, sidewalks, weeds, litter, and ladybugs. Location descriptions may be as simple as "in front of the school," "in a tree," or "on the sidewalk."

Natural Things
- Grass - Robin
- Trees - Ant

Manufactured Things
- Paper
- Sock
- Bottle cap
- Gum wrapper

3. Return to the classroom, and review the Discovery Charts. Ask, "Did we find everything we expected to find? Are there any things we need to add to our charts?" Add the additional items the children found.

4. Help the children create a record of their observations. See the example below or the "What's in Our Environment?" Discovery Page, or have the class create a database on a computer. Encourage them to add to their record throughout the unit.

N = Natural	M = Manufactured	
Date	Where We Looked	What We Found
Oct. 10	Sandbox	Ⓝ Beetle, Cap Ⓜ, Twig Ⓝ
Oct. 11	Front lawn	Ⓜ Can, Grass Ⓝ, Ants Ⓝ

The children could compare their list to a list made by another class or the previous year's class. If you generate a database on the computer, you may want to use it to help the children create graphs of such things as the number of different plants found in the school yard compared to the number of different animals.

5. Help the children create a map or three-dimensional representation of the school yard. If they need assistance getting oriented, you may want to lay out the basic framework, including the school buildings and paved areas. Once the framework is in place, have the children draw or make models of the things they observed and put them in the appropriate places.

Assessing the Activity

Are the children aware that a multitude of organisms and manufactured materials make up their environment? Can they name some of the natural and manufactured things they observed in the environment?

Additional Stimulation

Sharing Surveys—If the children have conducted surveys with their families of their backyards or neighborhoods, have them share their lists with the class. Talk with them about how their various findings compare and how the backyard and school-yard environments are the same and different.

Let's Help Out—To stimulate interest in the environment, you may want to have the children plan a class project to plant trees or a garden or to design, construct, and hang bird feeders.

What Lives Here?—Bring in several hula hoops. Explain that each Discovery Group will take a hoop to the school yard and roll it out to fall on a spot on the lawn. Then each group will try to identify and count all the kinds of plants and animals inside their hoop—for example, two kinds of grass, a clover, a dandelion, a plant with tiny stickers, two kinds of ants, a beetle, and a grasshopper. You could ask them to tape a cutting of each plant in their Discovery Journals. Before they remove the hoop, have them compare and share observations with other groups. The lawn is just one environment in the school yard and will probably contain a relatively small variety of organisms; the children might survey other nearby environments for comparison.

Environment Museum—Have the children collect some of their findings—dried leaves, a discarded candy wrapper, a snake skin—for a classroom museum. They should label each item with the location in which it was found, its name (if they know it), and any other information they think would be interesting to someone who visits their museum.

Handmade Viewfinders—A paper-cup survey will allow the children to conduct a general scan of their environment. Prepare cups by removing the bottoms and punching a hole on each side of one end. String a piece of yarn through the holes and tie it. Have the children stand back from the edge of a field or woods. As they look through the open cup, have them line up the yarn running through the center with the bottom of the field or woods or at the horizon. This divides the viewing area into two fields. This unique viewfinder will help focus the children's observations and give them another way to describe the location of the plants and animals they see in the environment. Ask them about the observations they are making: what they see above and below the dividing line, what living things they see in each section, which area contains more colors, and so on.

Seeing All Around Us—Have children gather in groups of four and stand with their backs facing each other, each child looking in a different direction. Ask them to look straight ahead as they each describe what they see from their viewpoint, sharing observations and descriptions.

Who's Along Our String?—Help the children to survey their environment using a long piece of string, which allows the study of a variety of environments at one time. Lay out a length of string, perhaps having it traverse a sidewalk, a walking path, and a patch of grass. Have several groups work along a single string, counting and describing all the plants and animals that they discover along it.

Environment Quilt—Have the children tie the corners of 16 or 20 plastic bags together with yarn. They can place one of the objects they found on the playground into each bag, creating a connected, quiltlike wall hanging.

Through Our Window—Choose a window in the classroom, and create a class journal to keep at the window. Children can add to the journal drawings and descriptions of whatever they happen to see through the window—plants, animals, and other objects—at various times of the day and over a period of weeks.

Let's Be Soil Scientists

Most of us don't often think about the dirt beneath our feet unless we're planting flowers or trying to keep our shoes clean—or if we're farmers who make a living from growing crops. If we had to depend on the food we grew to feed our families, we would probably pay closer attention to soil. In this activity, the children study soil samples and learn that not all soil is the same.

CONNECTIONS

TO LANGUAGE

The Discovery Journals—The children record their observations and descriptions of soil samples in their Discovery Journals.

Expressive Language—The children develop an operational definition for the word *soil*.

TO THE FAMILY

The soil-examining procedures that the children learn in this activity will be fun to apply at home. Talk with the children about the procedures for collecting the samples so they can demonstrate them to their families. Place the samples the children bring in next to the ones collected from the school yard. Send home a note with the children:

Your child has been learning about the many types of soil. During the next couple of weeks, we'd like your child to spend some time looking for different kinds of soil.

You and your child may want to collect soil samples when you visit relatives or friends in another area or travel to other locations with different soil types. Help your child to place each sample in a plastic bag and label it with the name of the person who collected it, when it was collected, and where it was found. If you find any objects in the soil, remind your child to mention them in class so that they may be added to the class list of items that can be found in soil.

Science Process Skill

Focused Observation

Science Concept

Everything around us is part of our environment.

Science Vocabulary

clay

loam

moisture

names of objects found in the soil

sand

soil

test

Materials

garden trowels or a shovel

containers such as plastic cups or plastic bags *(for collecting soil samples)*

sieves

hand lenses

low-power microscope *(optional)*

photographs or illustrations of different types of soil *(optional)*

Before the Activity

Find several locations where the children will be able to dig to collect soil samples. If it is not possible for the children to collect their own samples at school, bring in containers of soil yourself (preferably from more than one site). If the children have already brought in samples from home, include those as well. When you or one of the children brings a sample to the classroom, make sure it is labeled with identifying information: who collected it, the date it was collected, and where it was found.

If possible, borrow a dissecting microscope (a low-power microscope that is easy to use and doesn't require special lighting) from a middle school or high school teacher.

What to Do

1. Take the children outside to collect a variety of soil samples in plastic or coated-paper cups, plastic bags, or other containers. If you are supplying the samples, let the children inspect them, and talk about where you found them.

2. Label the soil samples A, B, C, and so on, and place them where all the children can observe them. Ask the children to write several words in their Discovery Journals that describe each soil sample. You may also want to create a Discovery Chart of their descriptions in addition to (or instead of) the journal entries.

Soil Sample	Color	Texture	Smell	Type of Soil
A	gray	smooth	musty	
B	dark brown	rough crumbly	rich	
C				

3. Talk with the children about what they have already found or might find in soil. Then have them sift the soil through a sieve. They may find insects, worms, seeds, roots, rocks, metal, glass, plastic, and many other things. Talk about the different types of soils, such as sand, clay, and loam. You may want to locate photographs or illustrations of various types of soil to help the children compare their samples. Have the class determine what type of soil each sample is, and add this information to the Discovery Chart.

4. Place two types of soil side by side, and have the children observe the samples. Ask, "Do these look alike? How are they different? How are they the same?" Help them examine the soils more closely using hand lenses and a microscope, if one is available.

TYPES OF SOIL

Soil is produced when rocks are broken down by the process of weathering. Soil particles are related to the type of parent rock from which they came. Under normal conditions, it takes about 500 years to make a layer of soil 1 inch deep.

Sand results from erosion by glaciers, winds, oceans, and other moving waters and is primarily composed of quartz and feldspar.

Clay is usually produced by the intense weathering of rocks and is essential for growing crops because it holds moisture and prevents organic material from being washed away.

Loam, a mixture of sand, clay, and humus (decomposing plant and animal material), is among the richest agricultural soils.

Silt is usually the result of very fine clay particles carried by moving water and deposited in layers when the water stops moving, as in a lake or across a flood plain.

5. Help the children to operationally define the word *soil*. Lead a brainstorming session in which they talk about all they know about the characteristics of soil, and then help them to put their knowledge into words.

Assessing the Activity

Can the children use descriptive language to discuss the unique characteristics of the various soil samples?

Additional Stimulation

How Moist Is the Soil?—You may want to help your young scientists do some additional exploration of their soil samples. They can use cobalt chloride test strips, obtainable from science suppliers or secondary science teachers, to test the moisture content of the soil. These test strips indicate the presence of moisture by turning pink. Have the children start by moistening a small amount of a sample; then have them drop the sample onto a strip of test paper. Have them record the results for each soil sample. Explain that soils that retain moisture are better for plants and that farmers and scientists sometimes test soils to see how good they would be for growing food.

How Acidic Is the Soil?—Here is another optional soil test. The children can use litmus or pH paper, obtainable from science suppliers or secondary science teachers, to test the acidity of their samples. Most of the samples will register around 7 (neutral). Some will be slightly acidic (with a number less than 7) and others will be basic (with a number greater than 7). Explain that scientists test soil pH because some plants grow better in acidic soil and others grow better in basic soil.

Growability Test—Take the class to visit three or four of the sites where soil samples were taken. Have them plant grass seed

OPERATIONAL DEFINITIONS

An operational definition is a method of defining an object (in this case, soil) in a way that is inclusive of all the attributes and characteristics that are observed about it. It is used when people need a working agreement about what something is. For example, *liquid* might be operationally defined as any substance that is a fluid, can fill a container of any shape, and cannot be easily compressed.

or flower seed and observe the growth of the plants over several weeks. Talk with them about which soil sites are more productive, and what other factors—such as irrigation and sunlight—might affect the sprouting of seeds and the growth of plants.

Soil Paintings—Encourage self-expression by having the children create paintings using soil as the medium. Help them to mix water and soil, adding tempera paint for additional color. The children might glue rocks and other artifacts found in the soil to their paintings.

Mud Sculptures—Let the children make sculptures from different types of soil (for example, clay, sand, and humus-rich soil). Observe and discuss differences between the soils as the sculptures dry.

Soil Plugs—Use a bulb planter to gather plugs of different types of soils from various locations. Plunge the bulb planter into the soil. Remove it, and then turn the planter upside down and push the plug out, being careful to keep the sample in one piece. Place the sample in a clear container so the children can view the plug from all directions.

LEAD IN SOIL

Because of health concerns about lead levels in young children, avoid areas where lead might be present in the soil, such as where soil is exposed to leaded gas (as along roadways, especially near stop signs and gas stations) and near older buildings with peeling paint. Almost all houses built before 1960, and many built between 1960 and 1974, have leaded paint. You may want to share this information with parents.

What's Hidden in the Soil?

Soil is much more than just inert material: it is alive with all sorts of microscopic organisms. This activity is a simple way to demonstrate to children that there are things in the soil that we cannot see. With the help of a little water, children can stimulate the seeds that are often hidden in soil to begin the cycle of growth anew.

CONNECTIONS

 TO LANGUAGE

Discovery Journals—The children record their initial descriptions about what they think will happen to soil samples when water is added, and their observations as the experiment progresses, in their journals.

Discovery Chart—The children help create a daily record of the experiment on a class chart.

TO MATHEMATICS

Charting—The class develops a chart of the soil samples and how each responds to the addition of water.

Before the Activity

Collect soil samples for the class, perhaps having the children help. Draw samples from several locations, such as two areas of the school grounds, your own garden, the woods, and a planter. Label each sample with the location from which it was taken. Take topsoil where possible, as it is more likely than other soil to contain seeds that will germinate.

Prepare one sample of potting soil, which will not likely produce any sprouts because no viable seeds will be present.

Science Process Skill

Focused Observation

Science Concept

Everything around us is part of our environment.

Science Vocabulary

germinate

moisten

plant parts such as leaf, stem, and root

sprout

topsoil

Materials

outside soil *(taken from the top 1–3 cm)*

containers such as clear food tubs with lids or plastic bags

water

eyedroppers

radish, grass, or other small seeds

paper towels

hand lenses

measuring cups

microscope *(optional)*

potting soil *($\frac{1}{2}$ cup)*

What to Do

1. Put out the samples of soil, and have each Discovery Group choose a soil sample and fill their container with about half a cup of topsoil. Help the children label each container with the soil's origin. Ask them to carefully observe the soil with their hand lenses and to record all of their observations in their Discovery Journals.

2. Have groups use an eyedropper to add enough water to moisten the soil in their containers. The soil should be *moist*, not wet or muddy. As a control, help the class prepare a container of very dry soil to which no water is added.

3. As a class, place some radish, grass, or other small seeds into a resealable plastic bag. Slip a moistened and folded paper towel in with the seeds, and seal the plastic bag. Set this bag aside for the children to observe occasionally during the course of the experiment.

4. Help the children seal and store their containers. They must be stored at room temperature for seeds to sprout. Light is not necessary for sprouting, but appropriate temperature and moisture conditions are.

5. Talk with the children about where the samples were gathered and what they think might happen to them. Ask, "Will adding water cause any changes in our soil?" Have the children write or illustrate in their journals what they think will happen to the soil in their containers.

6. Over the next week or two, have the children make daily observations of the soil samples. When and if something happens, have them share their discoveries with the class and record and draw the information in their journals. Use a Discovery Chart to create a daily record of what is happening in the various soil samples.

Soil Taken from	Day 1	Day 2	Day 3	Day 4	Day 5
Playground	nothing	nothing	2 tiny sprouts	4 sprouts	5 sprouts
Becky's backyard					
Flowerpot					

7. Call the children's attention to the seeds in the sealed bag. The children should see that the seeds have sprouted. This observation will serve as a frame of reference for the children to understand what is happening with their moistened soil samples.

8. Ask the children, "Where did the plants in your soil come from? Do you think there may have been seeds in your soil?"

9. After all the soil samples have had time to germinate, group the soils by those that contained seeds and those that did not. You might help the class try to find commonalties among the soils that contained seeds that germinated. Ask, for example, "Did garden soil or forest soil have more sprouts—meaning more seeds?" If one sample was potting soil, it should not have produced any sprouts because it will have been sterilized to kill any seeds present; explain this to the children. Then ask, "Why did we add water to the soil?"

Assessing the Activity

Do the children's journal entries include logical predictions for what might happen when the soil is moistened and an accurate account of what has happened? Can the children explain why no plants sprouted in the potting-soil sample?

Additional Stimulation

Growing Bare Spots—Soils are not the only determining factor in plant growth. Sometimes plants don't grow because the trampling of too many feet prevent them from doing so. Take a walk through the school yard with the children, asking them to look for areas where plants are not growing. Collect some soil from these bare spots, and try to sprout the seeds that may be present in the soil.

Comparing Soils—Some soils are better than others for growing things. Have the children try to grow a particular type of seed in a variety of soils to test whether some of the soils produce better plants than others.

Fungi Garden—Help the children create fungi gardens by adding small samples of soil to petri dishes containing unflavored gelatin. Follow the directions on the gelatin box to make a thick liquid, and fill the bottom of the petri dishes (or other small plastic containers, such as margarine tubs) with the gelatin. Sprinkle the soil samples over the gelatin, and allow the dishes to sit at room temperature for several days. Keep the dishes uncovered, and make sure that you and the children wash your hands after handling the dishes. *Caution:* Some children may be allergic or at least susceptible to irritation from exposure to bacteria and fungi that might grow in the soil samples. Take care that the children avoid direct contact with the petri dishes by having them wear rubber gloves when handling the dishes. Keep the dishes in an area separate from the classroom. Any children who suffer from allergies or show signs of red or teary eyes should leave the area when they feel discomfort.

THE GERMINATION OF A SEED

A seed is covered by a tough outer seed coat. Inside is a young plant, or embryo, and enough stored food to sustain the new plant during and after germination.

The germination of a seed begins with the uptake of water, which greatly increases the volume of the seed. The presence of water begins the process of rapid cell division, and the growing embryo soon bursts through the seed coat. The root heads in the direction of gravity, and the shoot, which will become the above-ground part of the new plant, heads toward the surface.

Starting Over—Help the children collect the humus that is formed by a rotting log, as is often found on a forest floor. Have them plant an acorn or maple seed in the soil, add water, and watch what happens. The children can then write a story about what might happen to a tree after it dies.

Mixed Soil—Just for fun, have the children mix all the types of soil they have worked with together to grow a special class plant, such as a sunflower. As they watch to see how large their plant will grow, have them develop a way to record the growth.

A Deep-Soil Garden—Have the children grow some garden plants in two containers: one filled with soil taken from deep below the surface (perhaps from a construction site), and one filled with potting soil. Have them measure the differences in the growth of the plants over time, and talk about what may be causing the differences.

A Look at What We Breathe

Air contains the elements that all living things depend upon for their survival. Polluted air has negative effects on all life on Earth. This activity helps the children visualize the pollution that may be present in the air they breathe and explore some of the things they might do about it.

CONNECTIONS

 TO LANGUAGE

Expressive Language—The children talk about the differences they observe in the air quality of various locations and share their ideas about what can be done to curb air pollution.

 TO THE FAMILY

The search for air pollutants can continue in the children's homes. Send home a note with the children, along with small pieces of contact paper:

Your child has been learning about the air we breathe. We'd like you and your child to continue this study in your home. Your child will show you what to do with the contact paper. Please help with placing the pieces of contact paper, sticky side up, in locations around your house. After one week, your child can bring the results to school to share with the class. Also, if you have time, please show your child the air filter in an air conditioner or furnace, and talk with him or her about what you see.

Before the Activity

Purchase clear contact paper, which is available in rolls in variety and hardware stores. Cut at least one piece of contact paper for each Discovery Group.

Science Process Skill

Guided Inference

Science Concept

We can observe and cause changes in our environment.

Science Vocabulary

air

impurity

pollution

Materials

clear contact paper *(1 piece per group)*

permanent markers

tape

pushpins

container with lid

hand lenses

microscope *(optional)*

What to Do

1. Have each Discovery Group select a location in or around the school to place a piece of clear contact paper, sticky side up. Encourage them to be creative as they choose their spots. Try the classroom windowsill, the boiler room, the principal's office, the teachers' lounge, and the playground. Help the children label each piece of contact paper with its location using a permanent marker and secure it with tape or push-pins. You may want them to make a "Do Not Touch" sign for each site. As a control, have the class place a piece of contact paper in a covered container.

2. Leave the contact paper exposed to the air for a week. Then let the groups bring the pieces of contact paper back to the classroom and display them in a central location.

3. Have the groups examine the pieces of contact paper. Ask, "What differences, if any, do you see in the clearness of the various pieces of contact paper? Are they as clean as they were when we started? Which location had the cleanest air? Which had the dirtiest air?" Provide a new piece of contact paper for comparison, and also let the children examine the contact paper that was kept in the closed container. Hand lenses or a microscope will help them examine the contact paper more closely. They might also try placing the sticky sides of the contact paper on white paper to increase the contrast and visibility.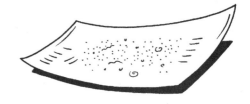

4. Discuss things in the school and the community that might contribute to local air pollution, such as smoking, car exhaust, fire, smoke from industry, spray of pesticides or fertilizers, and wind-borne soil or dust.

5. Talk with the children about their ideas of ways to keep our air clean.

Assessing the Activity

Does the children's discussion indicate an understanding that the particles collected on the contact paper were once suspended in the air, which they breathe? Are they able to identify some sources of air pollution and some ways they might help keep the air clean?

Additional Stimulation

Clean-Air Campaign—Have the children create posters with pictures and messages that discourage pollution. They may want to brainstorm a class slogan for the posters. The posters can be hung at school and out in the community. Encourage the children to compose a letter to the principal or a government official about their findings and concerns. This might also be a good time to invite someone from the Environmental Protection Agency (a government agency that monitors water and air quality and the conditions of other natural resources), the American Lung Association, or a related agency to speak to the class about pollution. If speakers aren't available, these organizations or the local health department will likely be able to suggest some appropriate videos. As part of the clean-air campaign, the children could list the places in their community (businesses, intersections, and so on) where they see air pollution taking place, and even take photographs or draw pictures of each location.

Window Washers—Wash the outside of two adjacent windows. Continue to wash one of the windows on a regular basis, but not the other. Have the children compare the appearance of the two windows over a period of time. One will remain clean while the other grows dirty, indicating that there are particles in the air that become attached to the glass.

Dust in the Wind—Point out to the children the dust particles visible in a beam of sunlight or the light from a flashlight. With the room darkened, ask, "Where does all that dust come from? What do you think happens when we breathe the dust?" Make the effect more dramatic by clapping two chalk erasers together or shaking a blanket in the beam of light. Discuss with the children how our noses filter the air we breathe.

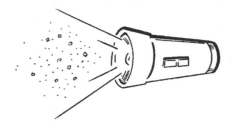

Tales of the Environment—Have the children make up stories and write books using super heroes, cartoon characters, or themselves as campaigners for clean air and fighting the "villains" (such as pollutants or polluters). Or they could write a story about what people might have to do to survive if the air, water, and soil become very polluted.

Life Around the World—Find pictures in magazines that demonstrate the different levels of air quality in a variety of geographical locations, such as a mountain scene and a heavily polluted city scene. Have a class discussion about what causes air pollution and how it might affect the people living in it. Ask, "What would it be like to live in a place with very clean air? What would it be like to live in a place with very polluted air?"

Filtering the Air—Many people have small air cleaners or filters in their homes, cars, or furnaces. Ask families to put a used air filter into a plastic bag and allow their children to bring it to school to share with the class. The children can explain where the filters came from and what they do.

Adding Up Raindrops

Like air, water is a necessity for all living things. Rain and snow gauges help us measure the amount of precipitation that reaches the ground, and weather forecasters use other special equipment to determine how much rain or snow has fallen in a given place over a given time. This activity lets the children make their own rain or snow gauges to measure the amount of moisture that has fallen at school and at home.

CONNECTIONS

TO LANGUAGE

Discovery Journals—The children record their daily findings in their journals or on the "Rainfall Chart."

Written Language—The children may write a letter to a weather forecaster or meteorologist.

TO MATHEMATICS

Measurement—The children measure the amount of rainfall collected using their rain gauges.

Addition—The children add up the daily rainfall amounts to find the total rainfall over a period of time.

 TO THE FAMILY

Observations of precipitation can also be made at home. Send home a note with the children:

Your child has been learning about precipitation in the form of snow and rain. We'd like you and your child to continue exploring this topic. For one week, please take time to follow the weather report in the newspaper or on television with your child. Keep a daily log of weather information such as temperature, rainfall, wind speed, and wind direction.

Before the Activity

Send a letter home with your students requesting that families donate containers for the rain-gauge activity, such as clear plastic cups, baby-food jars, sour-cream containers, and margarine tubs. If possible, arrange for a weather forecaster or meteorologist to visit the class and talk about his or her profession, and bring in

Science Process Skill

Focused Observation

Science Concept

We can observe and cause changes in our environment.

Science Vocabulary

centimeter
compare
less, more
measure
meteorologist
rain gauge
rainfall
weather forecaster

Materials

small containers such as plastic cups, margarine containers, and baby-food jars *(for collecting precipitation)*

permanent marker *(optional)*

metric rulers or the "Rain-Gauge Rulers" Discovery Page *(optional; copy the master on page 84 onto transparency film)*

"Rainfall Chart" Discovery Page *(optional; see page 85)*

some books that will help the children answer their weather questions. If you decide to use the "Rain-Gauge Rulers" Discovery Page, photocopy the master onto transparency film and cut out the rulers.

What to Do

1. Ask the children, "Why do you think we need rain?" Record their responses on a Discovery Chart. Discuss how all living things need water to live. "Where does water go after it falls to the ground? What do you think might happen if we get too little or too much rainfall?" You may want to mention recent weather events, such as flooding, a hot spell, or a heavy storm.

2. Ask, "How do we know how much rain or snow has fallen? Who tells us?" Talk about what meteorologists do and about weather reports in the newspaper and on radio and television. Ask, "How do weather forecasters know how much rain has fallen?"

3. To answer this question, and any other questions the children have about precipitation, invite a meteorologist to visit the classroom. The class could write a letter to a local meteorologist asking for weather information or explanations for any unanswered questions. Resources may be available on the Web; weather videos and weather channels are also good resources. You might also make several books on the topic available to the children. The children will learn that meteorologists use special measuring equipment to measure how much precipitation has fallen in a given period of time.

How Living Things Use Water

to drink

to keep cool

for protection

to float

to swim

to wash

4. Say, "Now we are going to make our own rain measurers that are like the rain gauges that weather forecasters use!" Give each Discovery Group a small container, and have them place the containers in an area of the school yard where they will not be disturbed. You may want to help them label their containers using a permanent marker.

5. After each rainfall, have the children use metric rulers or "Rain-Gauge Rulers" to measure the depth of the precipitation in their rain catchers and record the information in their Discovery Journals or on the "Rainfall Chart." The containers should be emptied after each rain. By adding the various amounts of rainfall, the children can determine the total rainfall over a period of time, such as a week, a month, or even the entire school year.

6. If some children have used their rain gauges at home, have them bring in their results to compare with the class's results. There may be differences due to collection and measurement errors, so you may want to talk about sampling techniques with the class. If differences might be due to scattered showers, talk about this as well.

7. Let the children compare their daily findings to actual weather reports. Ask, "Are they the same or nearly the same? What might be the reason for big differences?"

8. Save the rain gauges for use in Activity 11.

Assessing the Activity

Are the children's records of the amounts of precipitation reasonably consistent with your findings? Can they give reasons for a rain gauge being a valuable tool? Are they able to explain differences between their readings and readings taken at other locations?

Additional Stimulation

Technically Speaking—Have the children use rulers and permanent markers to calibrate their rain gauges for future use.

Let's Make a Rainfall Map—Enlarge a map of the area (possibly from the local telephone book) so that each child can indicate the precipitation amounts measured at various locations. Compare the rainfall from the different locations on the map. This could lead to a discussion about the difference between area-wide thunderstorms and scattered showers.

Gauging a Snowfall—If you are lucky enough to have a snowfall during this unit, let the children stick rulers into the snow to measure the amount that fell. About 10 centimeters of snow will melt to produce 1 centimeter of water. Have the children collect a container of snow, measure its depth, and then allow it to melt and measure the depth of the resulting water.

Rain Here, There, and Yonder—Obtain an annual rainfall map, and help the children compare rainfall in your community to other locations on the map.

Weather Scrapbook—Have the children clip weather maps, weather predictions, and weather reports from the daily newspapers to make a scrapbook over a period of a month. Their collected data can be used as the basis of math lessons, in which they can compare, add, subtract, and average the data.

Raindrop Art—Have the children add patches of color to sheets of paper, using water-soluble coloring or painting materials. Allow the creations to dry. Then place them in the rain on a flat surface, and let the children watch the patterns that develop.

Check the Sprinkler—How many centimeters of water fall during the time a sprinkler runs? Have the children check this out with their rain gauges. After they investigate, ask them whether a sprinkler is a substitute for real rain.

Statuary Rain Gauges—Have the children decorate the outsides of their rain gauges with plaster of Paris or another solid casting material. They can create rain-measuring statues for the garden, such as vases, mushrooms, and turtles.

Clean, Clear Water

Would we drink water straight from a muddy river? Probably not. One of the things that we can change in our environment is the quality of the water we drink. We usually treat the water we take from rivers, oceans, lakes, reservoirs, and underground sources before we use it in our homes because it often contains harmful parasites and contaminants. In this activity, the children explore a method of cleaning water that is similar to the process used in municipal water-filtration systems.

CONNECTIONS

 TO LANGUAGE

Discovery Journals—The children draw their impressions of the filtering process and use their writing skills to explain, at their own level, how the system works.

 TO MATHEMATICS

Measurement—The children measure the layers of material they use to make water filters.

Before the Activity

The filters that the children create in this activity will take some time and preparation on your part, but are well worth the effort. However, if you lack the time or materials, very simple water-filtration systems can be made by substituting coffee filters for the cotton, charcoal, and sand.

To prepare for the activity, crush the charcoal briquettes—about three per group—by placing them in a double paper bag and hitting the bag with a hammer. Create a poster-size water filter "recipe card" by drawing and labeling the layers that make up the filter.

Cut the tops from half of the plastic soda bottles; the children will use the tops as funnels and the bottoms as containers. Each Discovery Group will also need an intact soda bottle.

Science Process Skill

Focused Observation

Science Concept

We can observe and cause changes in our environment.

Science Vocabulary

clean
clear
filter
germs
impurities
pure
purify
remove
water-treatment plant

Materials

2-liter plastic soda bottles with lids *(2 per group)*

water

soil

tablespoons

cotton balls

clean sand

crushed charcoal briquettes

cups *(1 per group)*

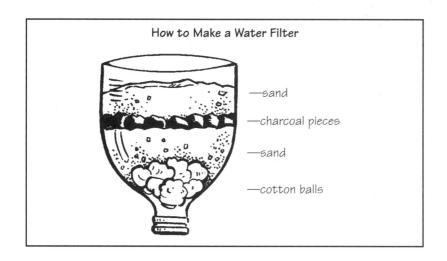

How to Make a Water Filter

—sand

—charcoal pieces

—sand

—cotton balls

What to Do

1. Talk with the children about the fact that most cities have water-treatment plants that clean or purify the drinking water. Talk about any home water-filtering systems the children are familiar with and whether some families drink bottled water. Explain, "The water is dirty when it comes to the

water plant. If we drink dirty water, we could become sick or get diseases. Part of the cleaning process is called *filtering*. We are going to filter some dirty water to see what this procedure is and how it works."

2. Have each Discovery Group fill a 2-liter plastic bottle three-fourths full of water. Direct each group to add about 1 tablespoon of soil to the water, place the lid on the bottle, and shake the bottle vigorously to make muddy water.

3. Have the children place the inverted "funnels" in the bottom halves of the bottles. Help them to prepare their filters by layering materials in the funnels in the following order:

   - Spread a layer of cotton in the bottom of the funnel about 5 centimeters thick.

   - Add about 5 centimeters of sand.

   - Place the equivalent of about three crushed charcoal briquettes on the sand.

   - Add another 3-centimeter layer of sand.

4. Once the layers are in place, have the children pour some clean water through their filters to help compact the materials.

5. Have groups again vigorously shake their bottles of muddy water to be sure they are well mixed.

6. Have each group pour a cup of muddy water through their filter. Say, "Watch the filtered water as it trickles into the bottom of the bottle. Is it cleaner? Do you think it's OK to drink?" Help the children understand that even if the water looks clean, their filters will still leave impurities in the water that can't always be seen. Explain that water-cleaning plants add chemicals to filtered water to kill the remaining germs.

7. Ask the children to compare the filtered water to the muddy water. Ask, "How are the muddy water and the filtered water different?" Suggest that the children be sure to smell and look, but caution them not to drink the water.

8. In their Discovery Journals, have the children draw their filter at work cleaning the dirty water. Encourage them to use their own words to describe how the filter works.

9. Have the children continue to pour muddy water through the filter. Say, "Look at the water filter now. Is its appearance changing? How?"

Assessing the Activity

Can the children explain how the filter helps to clean dirty water? Can they explain what happened to the tablespoon of dirt that they had originally added to their bottle of clean water?

Additional Stimulation

Cleaning Up Pond Scum—Have the children collect some pond water or water from local lakes and creeks and try to filter it with the filter they made in the activity. They can use a microscope to look for impurities and living organisms in the water samples before and after filtering them. Another fascinating activity is to have them use a microscope to observe these water samples every other day or so for a couple of weeks to see what is changing. They can make sketches of what they see and compare their drawings over a period of time.

A Good Pool Is a Clean Pool—If possible, have someone bring in a sample of water from a clean swimming pool and from a pool that has been sitting unattended for a while. Help the children to observe the differences between the two samples. Talk with them about how the pool water may have become contaminated and what can be done to clean it. Let the children test whether their filters can help clean the dirty pool water.

Field Trip—Take the children to the city water plant so they can observe how their drinking water is purified, or have a representative visit the class to talk with the children about the process.

How Does Water Get Dirty?—Begin a chain story, and have the children add to it: *One bright day, a dark cloud came over our town, and it began to rain. The raindrops that fell on the children were made of clean, pure water, but. . . .* Give each child a turn to add to the story, telling where the water from the raindrops went and what happened to it. The children may mention the fact that even rainwater is not truly pure and add ideas about what else may be in rainwater.

Taste Test—Bring in several kinds and brands of bottled water—including tap water, perhaps from the school fountain and from your home—and have the children do a taste test. Give each child a paper cup, and pour one sample, designated by letter or number, at a time. Have the class rate each sample or write something about it in their journals. Then reveal the sources of the water and let the class share their impressions.

Was It Here or Was It Made?

Some of the things we observe in the world around us are part of the creativity of nature; others are manufactured by human beings. This activity will help the children begin to differentiate between what nature produces and what is manufactured through human invention and ingenuity.

CONNECTIONS

 TO LANGUAGE

Expressive Language—The children share their observations about natural and manufactured objects in the environment. They write and attach labels identifying their school-yard collections and will indicate whether the objects are natural or manufactured.

 TO MATHEMATICS

Sorting and Classifying—The children sort and classify items into the categories *natural* and *manufactured*.

Before the Activity

Collect a few examples of natural and manufactured objects to stimulate discussion. For example, you might bring in a tree branch and a small piece of lumber, a log cut for firewood and a pressed fire log, and a chunk of rock and a piece of cut stone.

What to Do

1. Explain to the class that both natural and manufactured materials are part of our environment. Ask, "What is the difference between a *natural* object and a *manufactured* object? Let's look at some examples." Show the examples you have brought, and encourage the children to talk about them, especially their similarities and differences. Help the children develop operational definitions of *manufactured objects* as anything made by people and *natural objects* as materials that have not been made or processed by people.

2. Tell the children that they will be searching the area near the school for other examples of natural and manufactured objects to bring back to the classroom. Ask, "Before we go

Science Process Skill

Observing to Classify

Science Concept

Everything around us is part of our environment.

Science Vocabulary

collection

manufacture

nature, natural

Materials

examples of natural and manufactured objects *(see "Before the Activity")*

poster board, sticks, markers, and other sign-making materials

clear contact paper or plastic bags *(optional)*

boxes or other containers *(for collecting and sorting the items)*

on our search, what *natural* objects do you think we will find? What *manufactured* objects might we find?" On a Discovery Chart, make two lists of the items the children suggest.

3. Assign each Discovery Group to a separate area of the school grounds. Take the groups outdoors to show them their territories. Explain that each group is responsible for collecting items from their area and keeping it as litter-free as they can.

4. Bring the groups inside, and have each group design a sign to post in their area. Laminate the signs or cover them with clear contact paper or plastic bags to weatherproof them. Help the groups post their signs in their territories.

What We Might Find	
Natural	Manufactured
sticks	paper
flowers	can
grass	gum wrapper
rocks	plastic
soil	

5. Over the next week, have the groups collect natural and manufactured items from their areas. Caution them about picking up broken glass or other items that might be harmful. Help each group sort their collections into natural and manufactured items using separate boxes.

6. Have the children write and attach labels identifying their collections and indicating whether the objects are natural or manufactured. As an option, help groups make Venn diagrams by drawing circles on paper and sorting items into natural and manufactured categories. Objects that have aspects of both categories, such as a stone on a pendant, would be placed in the overlapping area.

7. Have groups display their collections. If the children disagree about how to categorize an item, encourage them to talk about how and why they made their decisions. The children's reasoning may vary. For example, is a piece of limestone from a driveway natural or manufactured (considering that it has been crushed to form gravel)?

8. Talk with the children about the litter they have collected. Ask, "How do you feel about finding litter around our school? Where did the litter come from?" Brainstorm ideas with the children for reducing litter, and choose at least one idea to implement. The groups may also be interested in adopting their areas for the entire year, just like companies and organizations "adopt" sections along the highway to help keep them litter-free.

9. Have the children return the natural objects to the environment and, if possible, recycle the manufactured objects (or save them for the Activity 8).

Assessing the Activity

Talk with the children about their rationales for sorting the various objects. Are they consistent with their classifications?

Additional Stimulation

Hanging Around—Offer the children a collection of magazines from which to cut pictures of manufactured and natural items. They may glue the pictures on cardboard to create collages or hang them from coat hangers to make mobiles.

Read the Labels—Ask the children to check the labels of their clothing to find out whether what they are wearing is made from natural or synthetic fibers. Create a Discovery Chart listing the fabrics that the children discover, such as cotton, wool, polyester, rayon, silk, and blends. If possible, attach samples of the various kinds of fabric.

Natural vs. Manufactured Snacks and Foods—With the class, investigate the school lunch menu for a whole week. Talk with the children about the ways in which some foods are processed. Discuss which foods are highly processed, which are unprocessed, and which are in between. Talk about how manufacturing plays a large role in the production of foods that the children consume.

Litter Blitz—Have the children line up at the edge of the playground or another designated area (perhaps just after recess or lunch, when there is likely to be more litter). Challenge them to see how much litter they can collect in a minute or two.

Let's Sort Some More—Help the children to further classify the manufactured objects they have collected by sorting them into groups with common characteristics, such as plastic, paper, glass, rubber, and metal. As a class, count the number of items in each group of manufactured objects and create a simple bar graph of the data. If the number of objects is small, the children can create a real graph by gluing the items on poster board.

Manufactured Things We Found

Metal	Plastic	Paper	Glass
staple			
penny			
nail	pen		
wire	bag		
dime	straw	wrapper	

Litter Alert—Have the children write letters to the principal, or an article for the school newsletter, explaining what they discovered about litter near the school.

Litter Sculpture—Take a large piece of chicken wire and freeform a sculpture skeleton—a large globe, a cube, or something more creative like a fish or bird. Show the children how they can push the pieces of trash they have collected into the chicken wire. Eventually, the skeleton can be covered with the litter collected by the class. Alternatively, sculptures can be created by attaching pieces of collected litter to one another using tape, string, and wire. The children could also glue their litter collections onto poster board. The sculptures or posters could be displayed for other students and teachers to see what was found on the school grounds.

The Truth About Trash

Our world is filled with billions of tiny organisms called *decomposers*. These creatures help clean our environment by breaking down much of what we discard as garbage. Unfortunately, some of the things we throw away cannot be decomposed. Our piles of waste are often so enormous that microorganisms cannot penetrate deeply into them. Decomposers require oxygen to function, so it is important not to overload landfills to the point that oxygen is unavailable to them. In this activity, the children will explore the importance of everyone's assistance in the care of our environment.

CONNECTIONS

 TO LANGUAGE

Written Language—The children record their predictions and observations about which materials will decompose and which will not.

Before the Activity

Gather a collection of items. Include items that are biodegradable, such as apple cores, lettuce, bread, leaves, grass, paper, and plants. Also gather items that are not biodegradable, such as small pieces (about a centimeter square) of metal, glass, plastic, cellophane, and fast-food containers; you can use many of the items found by the children in Activity 7. You will need enough items for every Discovery Group to have three or four biodegradable items and three or four non-biodegradable items.

Prepare a demonstration with one biodegradable item and one non-biodegradable item. Place about half a cup of soil into each of two bowls. To the first bowl add a biodegradable object, such as an apple core. To the second bowl add a non-biodegradable object, such as a piece of plastic. Pour three or four ounces of water into each bowl, and add enough soil to cover the objects.

Science Process Skill

Organizing and Communicating Observations

Science Concept

We can help take care of our environment.

Science Vocabulary

biodegradable

compost

decompose, decomposition

moisture

recycle

rotten

Materials

biodegradable and non-biodegradable items *(see "Before the Activity")*

2 bowls

water

plastic bags *(resealable, or with twist ties or rubber bands)*

about 1 liter of soil *(not sterilized potting soil)*

eyedroppers

plastic straws

tape

What to Do

1. After several days, unearth the objects you have buried, and show the children what has happened. Say, "A few days ago, I buried an apple core in this bowl and a plastic car in this bowl. Let's see if anything has happened to them." Unearth the objects, and let all the children see what has happened. "What do you notice? What has happened to the plastic car? What has happened to the apple core?" Introduce the concepts *biodegradable* and *decompose* as you talk about what happened to the biodegradable item.

2. Share the collection of objects with the children. Let the children classify the items into two groups—those they think will biodegrade and those they think will not biodegrade. Record their ideas on a Discovery Chart.

Will biodegrade	Won't biodegrade
cracker	nail
grapes	leaves
candy	marble

3. Have each Discovery Group label a plastic bag with their names and then place about a cup of soil in the bag. Let groups choose several items from the collection to put in the bag, including some they think will decompose and some they think will not. Ask them to list the objects they choose in their Discovery Journals and to draw how they think each object will look after several days.

4. Have groups add a small amount of water to their bags using an eyedropper; the soil should be damp, not muddy. Have them partially seal the bags, leaving a small opening, and then insert a straw about an inch into the opening and seal the top of the bag with tape. The straw will provide ventilation, allowing oxygen to enter. Sealing the bag will keep the moisture from evaporating too fast.

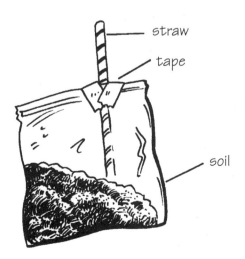

straw

tape

soil

5. Place the bags in a location where the children can observe them on a regular basis and occasionally mix the contents. After several days, you may want to label the bags and put them away to be observed periodically over a longer period of time. If the contents are composting properly, the bags will feel warm. Have the children record their observations in their journals. *Note:* Some objects will start decomposing immediately. For others, days or even weeks may pass before there is noticeable change.

6. Discuss composting with the children. Talk about the tiny organisms in the soil, called *microbes,* that are eating some of the buried materials. Ask the children, "What do you think microbes will be more likely to eat, apple cores or plastic?"

7. Ask, "What does your experiment tell you about litter? If materials that do not decompose are not good for our environment, what can we do to keep them from being thrown away? How can we reuse or recycle them?"

Assessing the Activity

Do the children's discussions and journal entries indicate their understanding that some litter is biodegradable and some is not? Can the children use the term *decompose?*

Additional Stimulation

Studying a Landfill—After the children's interest in the plastic bags has waned, take the bags outside and dump all of the individual samples into one large pile. Stand a plastic ruler in the center of the pile. Have the children observe their "landfill" frequently, observing any changes such as whether the pile shrinks over time. When they notice that the pile is getting smaller, ask them what they think is happening to the buried litter.

Buried Surprise—Wrap some of the collected items in a large piece of cheesecloth, and take the bundle to the school yard. Let the children use a shovel to dig a hole and bury the bundle in the soil. After three months, help the children dig up the bundle and examine the contents. What has happened? Which items have decayed or started to decay, and which haven't?

Barely Bread—Place a piece of moistened bread in a remote area of the playground, and cover it with a can or plastic container (to keep animals from disturbing it). After several days, uncover the bread, and allow the children to examine and record any changes that are taking place. Replace the container, and repeat the observations after several more days have passed.

Worm Food—Have the children construct a worm box from a wooden or plastic container; worms can be obtained from people who use worm boxes to compost at home or from commercial gardeners. The children can put discarded food from their snacks and lunches into the box.

Too Little, Too Much, Just Right—Place about a half cup of soil into several plastic bags. Add a biodegradable object, such as an apple core, to each bag. Add differing amounts of water to each bag, and let the children observe the bags periodically. After one week, take the objects from the bags and observe what has happened to them.

A Contract with Planet Earth

A *contract* is an agreement between two parties to do something. This activity puts into writing an agreement between the children and their families to do something that will serve to improve the environment in which we live.

CONNECTIONS

 TO LANGUAGE

Written Language—The children develop an environmental contract with the assistance of family members.

Discovery Journals—The children describe the outcome of the project in their journals.

 TO THE FAMILY

This activity involves the children's families in making a commitment to help protect the environment. Send a note home with the children:

Our class has spent the last several weeks learning about our environment. We have talked often about the role that all the people who live on our planet must play to help us maintain a quality of life that will allow future generations to live in a healthy, well-cared-for world.

As our unit comes to a close, it is important that the many things the children have learned about taking care of the environment not be forgotten. We would like to help the children put their new knowledge to use as lifelong habits.

Enclosed are two copies of an environmental contract. Please review the contract as a family, and feel free to add your own ideas to it. Have family members sign both copies. Post one in your home, and return the other to school with your child. Together we can make a difference.

Before the Activity

If you have reason to believe that the children are unlikely to get support from home with this project, consider developing a class project or a community volunteer activity instead. You might want to give children the option of choosing a class project or a family project.

Science Process Skill

Organizing and Communicating Observations

Science Concept

We can help take care of our environment.

Science Vocabulary

change

contract

environment

Materials

"Sample Environmental Contract" and "Environmental Contract" Discovery Pages *(optional; see pages 86 and 87)*

letter to families

What to Do

1. Brainstorm with the children some ideas about things they could do at home to care for their environment. Have the children record the ideas in their Discovery Journals, and list their ideas on the board.

2. Help the children to begin to write a contract to do something that will cause a positive change in the environment. Explain that the children will take their contracts home and finish working on them with their families. Some suggestions are growing house plants; walking or biking instead of using motorized transportation; recycling bottles, cans, and paper; cleaning up litter; and reducing use of packaging materials.

3. Send a list to families of projects they might undertake (see the "Sample Environmental Contract" Discovery Page); however, make it clear to the children and their families that *they* should come up with their own ideas. The sample contract should be accompanied by a letter of explanation that asks that the child bring a copy of the contract, signed by all family members, to the teacher.

4. Keep the contracts in a file, and periodically talk with the children about how their home environmental projects are going. Encourage the children to draw and write about their projects in their journals and to write thank-you notes to people who are helpful in fulfilling the contracts.

PROJECT IDEAS

A good class project might be to work out an agreement with a local business to supply the class with white paper that has been used on only one side. The children could use the reverse side for schoolwork.

A family project might be to agree that all lunches for a month will be brought to school in reusable containers.

Assessing the Activity

Do the children include information in their journals that demonstrates their awareness of how their projects impacted the environment?

Additional Stimulation

Environmental Pledge—Develop a class pledge to care for the environment. The children can brainstorm the pledge, and you can write it on the board for them to copy. The children can add artwork surrounding the pledge. Laminate what each child has made to make the pledges more durable, and send them home for sharing with the children's families.

Badges of Honor—Develop a certificate of appreciation that can be awarded to various classroom or individuals in the school that undertake a caring-for-our-environment activity.

People in the Environment—Invite a gardener, city planner, or landscape architect to talk with the class about the importance of green space and its effect on the environment. Invite a lawyer to talk about contracts and the important commitments they represent.

Adopt a Playground—Develop a plan for the class to assume responsibility for caring for and beautifying a specific section of the school grounds.

Thank You, Earth—Provide a frame for the children to create and illustrate poems about their world. This can be an individual, small group, or class activity. The children can add illustrations to their poems. Two sample poem frames follow.

Thank you, planet Earth.	*Our world is special.*
We love your green grass.	*We take care of our world.*
We love . . .	*We pick up trash.*
We love . . .	*We plant pretty plants.*
We love . . .	*We . . .*
Thank you, planet Earth.	*We . . .*
	We . . .
	We take care of our world.

Where's the Water?

Water is everywhere in our environment. Sometimes water's presence is obvious, as in a river or pond. Sometimes we just see evidence of water—we notice dew in the morning or condensation on our windows, or we sink into soggy grass, letting us know that water is hidden in the soil. Children probably don't realize all the different places water is present—even their bodies are 70 percent water!

CONNECTIONS

 TO LANGUAGE

Discovery Journals—The children write the names of the items they want to test for water content in their journals and record their findings after the testing.

 TO MATHEMATICS

Grouping—The children group objects by those that contain water and those that do not contain water.

Before the Activity

Gather a large collection of items to test for water's presence—for example, a tomato, a potato, dry rice, pasta, cereal, potato chips, salt, crackers, toast, bread, pretzels, a pencil, a crayon, orange peels, cotton balls saturated with oil, and vinegar and other liquids. Include a variety of items that obviously contain water, a variety of items that obviously don't contain water, and some items in which the presence or absence of water is not readily apparent.

Have enough items for each Discovery Group to be able to test at least five.

Science Process Skill

Guided Prediction

Science Concept

Everything around us is part of our environment.

Science Vocabulary

condensation

moisture

lake, marsh, ocean, pond, river, swamp, wetlands

Materials

collection of items to test for water content *(see "Before the Activity")*

resealable plastic bags

paper towels

Prepare a Discovery Chart by listing all the items you have collected, leaving space beside each to tally the groups' discovery.

Do They Contain Water?

apple	_____	vinegar	_____
pencil	_____	clay	_____
pretzels	_____	toast	_____
candy	_____	cereal	_____
crayon	_____	lemon	_____
rice	_____	oil	_____
cookie	_____	flower	_____
rubber band	_____	potato	_____
tomato	_____	orange peel	____

What to Do

1. Ask the children, "Where can we find water?" Discuss obvious sources such as ponds, lakes, oceans, streams, rain, and snow, and the fact that water is found in all of the living things in our world. Tell the children that they will be investigating to find things that contain water that we cannot see.

2. Ask each Discovery Group to choose five or more items from the collection you have prepared. Have them write the name of each item in their Discovery Journals. Be sure each group chooses some items that they expect to contain water and some they think won't. Ask the children why they think water is or is not present in a particular item. They may reply, for example, that a tomato or an orange drips when it is cut.

3. Have groups place each item in a resealable plastic bag, seal the bag well, and place it near a window. Let the sun shine on the bags for an afternoon. Water will evaporate from some of the items and condense on the sides of the bag. Condensation indicates the presence of water.

4. When condensation, or water drops, appears in the plastic bags, have the children remove the items and dry them with paper towels. Ask the children to record in their journals their observations of which items contained water. Then ask a member from each group to record their group's results on the class chart by making a tally next to the items that they discovered contained water.

As the plastic bag and its contents are warmed by the sun, some of the water in the enclosed items becomes water vapor. This moisture collects, or condenses, on the interior of the bag because it is in contact with the cooler outside air.

5. Now have the children choose additional items from the collection. Ask them to predict whether or not each item contains water, record the predictions in their journals, and repeat the experiment with the new items. The children should again record the results in their journals and tally their findings on the class chart. With enough experience, they should be able to predict which items do not contain enough water to form visible condensation on the plastic bag. (*Note:* There may be some water present even if no condensation is observable.)

6. In a follow-up discussion, reinforce the importance of water to all living things. Talk about the fact that humans can live for quite some time without food to eat, but only a short time without water. Help the children understand that water is an essential part of our environment.

Assessing the Activity

Can the children identify items that contain water? Can they describe a test they could conduct to determine whether water is present in something?

Additional Stimulation

Where Is the Water From?—Have the children tell or write creative stories about where the water in the various objects explored in the activity originated.

The Big Squeeze—Generate a class list of fruit juices, and ask the children to bring in various kinds of fruit. Make orange juice and lemonade, and then ask the children how the class might make grape juice, cherry juice, pineapple juice, or apple juice— or other kinds of juice from the fruit the children brought. Brainstorm ways to get the juice out of the fruit, and let the children try out their ideas. Talk with the children about what worked best. Were there any suggestions that didn't work? Why? Which fruits were the juiciest? You might have the children write in their journals about the activity or create a class book entitled *Making Juice!*

Up from the Soil—Have the children lay a plastic dropcloth over an area containing both living plants and concrete or other paving. After a short time, observe with them where water droplets have formed on the plastic and which covered areas contain little or no water. (Do not leave the plastic on the grass too long, or it will kill it.) Ask the children where the water is coming from.

Where Water Is Found—Have the children create a class poster of pictures cut from magazines to show the many places where water can be found.

Liquid from a Plant—Have the children gather leaves and stems from several different plants. If possible, include a succulent or two in the group. Help the children crush the plant material between two paper towels (perhaps having them lay a piece of wood over the towels and stand on it) and observe the amount of moisture that is collected.

Weather Watch

Weather has an immediate impact on children's lives: Will they play indoors or out? What clothing will they wear? This activity encourages the children to deepen their understanding of weather happenings through systematic observation and recording of weather conditions.

CONNECTIONS

TO LANGUAGE

Expressive Language—The children describe the weather conditions they observe.

TO MATHEMATICS

Measuring—The children use thermometers and rain gauges to measure weather conditions.

Charting—The children organize their predictions and observations into a weather chart.

Before the Activity

Videotape a weather report from the news, and set up a television and VCR to show the report in class. Make a weather chart for recording weather predictions and actual outcomes for each day of the month. Follow the model on the opposite page to make a one-month weather chart, or create a weather chart of your own design.

What to Do

1. Do this activity early in the morning when the children have a fresh memory of the weather conditions they experienced on the way to school. Show the recorded weather report, and discuss how television weather forecasters report the daily weather. Talk about the fact that forecasting is a difficult and important job. Ask, "Why is it helpful to know the weather forecast each day?" Explain that for the next couple of weeks, they will be looking at weather, recording weather data, and discussing weather conditions.

Science Process Skill

Guided Prediction

Science Concept

Everything around us is part of our environment.

Science Vocabulary

bar graph
cloud, cloud cover
compare
forecast
measure
observe
partly cloudy
predict
weather
wind

Materials

"Weather Symbols" Discovery Page *(optional; see page 88)*

rain gauges *(from Activity 5)*

videotape of a television news weather report

television and VCR

outdoor thermometers

One-Week Weather Chart

	Monday	Tuesday	Wednesday	Thursday	Friday
Date					
Today's Weather — Temperature: Precipitation: Cloud cover: Wind:					
Prediction of Tomorrow's Weather — Temperature: Precipitation: Cloud cover: Wind:					

2. Demonstrate how to read the outdoor thermometer. Depending on the experience of the group, you may choose to have them record the temperature in 5-degree increments or by single degrees. If necessary, review how to use and record the results of the rain gauge. Give the children the opportunity to practice these procedures, observing and offering instruction as needed.

3. Say, "We will take a few minutes at the end of each day to predict what we think the weather will be tomorrow." This will be a collaborative effort in that the children will discuss and come to a consensus vote, with your assistance, regarding four areas of weather forecasting:

- *Temperature:* hot, warm, cool, cold

- *Precipitation:* rain, snow, fog, none

- *Cloud cover:* clear, partly, mostly, completely cloudy

- *Wind:* calm, moderate, strong

4. Have the children make a prediction about the next day's weather. Have them indicate their forecast for the next day on the weather chart, perhaps recording their ideas by using these symbols:

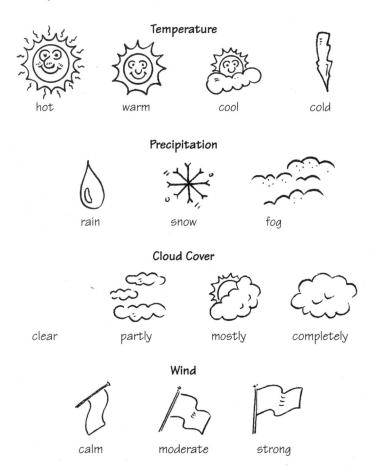

These symbols are reproduced on the "Weather Symbols" Discovery Page; you may want to have the children cut them out and affix them to the weather chart as they make predictions and record actual weather.

5. The next morning, have the children record the actual weather in the appropriate square. Once the class has grasped the procedure, individual groups can be assigned to perform the observations and make each day's forecast. The children will make Monday's prediction on a Friday. Ask them how well they do compared to the other days' predictions. Do they find making Monday's prediction easy?

6. After a period of time, have the children review the accuracy of their predictions along with the types of weather that have occurred recently. This is a good time to discuss the fact that weather forecasts are not always accurate.

Assessing the Activity

Are the children able to observe and communicate information about the weather and its effects on their daily lives? Do they understand the role of observation in predicting weather?

Additional Stimulation

Weather Log—The children can keep a log of their weather reports or reports clipped from news sources over an extended period of time.

What's Worn Where?—Have the children collect information about climates around the world and how clothing varies from one climate to another.

Our Weather Station—Have the children build a weather station that includes a thermometer, barometer, weather vane, and anemometer (a gauge for determining wind speed). There are many books available that include directions for adaptations of these instruments that children can make themselves or with minimal adult assistance. If available, show them a variety of manufactured weather instruments.

Daily Weather Forecast—Children can take turns giving the next day's local forecast. This can be made more exciting for them if you provide a microphone and a mock television set.

Summer Is a Time To . . . —Generate a class list of family and school activities that depend on the weather or season. Talk about how the weather affects what we wear as well as our plans for family and school activities. For example:

Winter	Spring	Summer	Fall
sledding	flying kites	swimming	hay rides
throwing snowballs	taking walks	picnics	picking pumpkins
ice skating	planting gardens	cookouts	collecting leaves

Let Me Tell You About My World

Encouraging children to become more aware of the environment is one way of developing their appreciation of the world in which they live. This activity gives them the opportunity to share what they have learned about the environment. At the simplest level, each child can illustrate and caption a page with information about the environment. Children with more experience can work in Discovery Groups, with each group choosing a topic to explore in depth.

CONNECTIONS

 TO LANGUAGE

> *Written Language*—The children write at their own level about a topic of their choice.

> *Expressive Language*—The children extend their expressive skills as they discuss what they have learned in this unit about the environment.

What to Do

1. Talk with the children about what they have discovered during this unit of study. Say: "Tell me about some of the things we have explored recently. What have you discovered about our environment?" You may want to review the Discovery Charts with them.

2. Ask, "How could we share our discoveries with other people?" Talk with the children about their ideas, and help them find a process that satisfies both their interests and their skills. Younger or less experienced children may want to each design a page for a class book, *What We Know About Our Environment*. Another class may want to work in Discovery Groups, with each group reporting on a topic in greater depth. They might create a poster, a scrapbook, or some other project to share their information and ideas.

Science Process Skill

Organizing and Communicating Observations

Science Concepts

We can help take care of our environment.

Science Vocabulary

connection

environment

vocabulary words from all previous activities

Materials

magazines with pictures

books about the environment

art supplies, including paper, colored pencils or markers, scissors, and glue

Discovery Pages from previous activities *(if students have used them)*

3. When the projects are complete, find a way to share them with others. The children could create a display for the school, share them at a parent meeting, or display them in a storefront, mall, or municipal building such as a library or city hall. A building principal or superintendent could also provide an appreciative audience.

A WORLD OF IDEAS

This activity is intended for the entire class to bring together and appreciate all of the work they have done in learning about the complexity and wonder of the environment. The projects and activities the children choose will paint a broad picture of where they have been and how you might guide them in continuing their exploration of the environment.

Assessing the Activity

Can the children describe their projects in a meaningful way?

Additional Stimulation

Let's Help Out—Using a Discovery Chart, have the children dictate what they have seen in the community that contributes to pollution and littering. After the list is complete, encourage the children to write a letter to the local newspaper editor explaining what they have observed and offering suggestions for improving the situation. The children can share and discuss their letters. Put all the letters into a booklet and mail them to the editorial department of the local newspaper.

An Environment for a Perfect World—Let your class brainstorm every thinkable way to make the Earth's environment a perfect place to live. Encourage them to dream about new and better ways to handle pollution, transportation, solid waste, and other issues. They might even suggest fantasy ideas, like a magic washing machine into which we can toss our environmental problems and have them come out clean.

What's in Our Environment?

Date	Natural Objects	Manufactured Objects	Location

© Addison Wesley Publishing Company/Published by Dale Seymour Publications®

Rain-Gauge Rulers

10 cm	10 cm	10 cm	10 cm	10 cm	10 cm	10 cm	10 cm
9 cm	9 cm	9 cm	9 cm	9 cm	9 cm	9 cm	9 cm
8 cm	8 cm	8 cm	8 cm	8 cm	8 cm	8 cm	8 cm
7 cm	7 cm	7 cm	7 cm	7 cm	7 cm	7 cm	7 cm
6 cm	6 cm	6 cm	6 cm	6 cm	6 cm	6 cm	6 cm
5 cm	5 cm	5 cm	5 cm	5 cm	5 cm	5 cm	5 cm
4 cm	4 cm	4 cm	4 cm	4 cm	4 cm	4 cm	4 cm
3 cm	3 cm	3 cm	3 cm	3 cm	3 cm	3 cm	3 cm
2 cm	2 cm	2 cm	2 cm	2 cm	2 cm	2 cm	2 cm
1 cm	1 cm	1 cm	1 cm	1 cm	1 cm	1 cm	1 cm

10 cm	10 cm	10 cm	10 cm	10 cm	10 cm	10 cm	10 cm
9 cm	9 cm	9 cm	9 cm	9 cm	9 cm	9 cm	9 cm
8 cm	8 cm	8 cm	8 cm	8 cm	8 cm	8 cm	8 cm
7 cm	7 cm	7 cm	7 cm	7 cm	7 cm	7 cm	7 cm
6 cm	6 cm	6 cm	6 cm	6 cm	6 cm	6 cm	6 cm
5 cm	5 cm	5 cm	5 cm	5 cm	5 cm	5 cm	5 cm
4 cm	4 cm	4 cm	4 cm	4 cm	4 cm	4 cm	4 cm
3 cm	3 cm	3 cm	3 cm	3 cm	3 cm	3 cm	3 cm
2 cm	2 cm	2 cm	2 cm	2 cm	2 cm	2 cm	2 cm
1 cm	1 cm	1 cm	1 cm	1 cm	1 cm	1 cm	1 cm

© Addison Wesley Publishing Company/Published by Dale Seymour Publications®

Rainfall Chart

Amount of Rainfall	Date	Container
10 cm 9 cm 8 cm 7 cm 6 cm 5 cm 4 cm 3 cm 2 cm 1 cm		
10 cm 9 cm 8 cm 7 cm 6 cm 5 cm 4 cm 3 cm 2 cm 1 cm		
10 cm 9 cm 8 cm 7 cm 6 cm 5 cm 4 cm 3 cm 2 cm 1 cm		
10 cm 9 cm 8 cm 7 cm 6 cm 5 cm 4 cm 3 cm 2 cm 1 cm		
10 cm 9 cm 8 cm 7 cm 6 cm 5 cm 4 cm 3 cm 2 cm 1 cm		
10 cm 9 cm 8 cm 7 cm 6 cm 5 cm 4 cm 3 cm 2 cm 1 cm		
10 cm 9 cm 8 cm 7 cm 6 cm 5 cm 4 cm 3 cm 2 cm 1 cm		

© Addison Wesley Publishing Company/Published by Dale Seymour Publications®

Sample Environmental Contract

Environmental Contract

We, the family of _____ ,
agree to support his or her efforts to help the environment by:

reducing, reusing, and recycling
returning glass bottles
growing houseplants, composting
wrapping presents in homemade paper
finding new uses for old things
giving away old things instead of throwing them out
picking up trash in our yard or the neighborhood
helping to clean a park or a beach
watering plants, planting a vegetable garden
growing flowers
quitting smoking

Signed _____

_____
family members

Signed _____
student

© Addison Wesley Publishing Company/Published by Dale Seymour Publications®

Environmental Contract

Environmental Contract

We, the family of _____ ,
agree to support his or her efforts to help the environment by:

Signed _____

_____
family members

Signed _____
student

© Addison Wesley Publishing Company/Published by Dale Seymour Publications®

Weather Symbols

Temperature

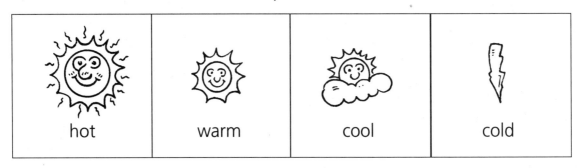

| hot | warm | cool | cold |

Precipitation

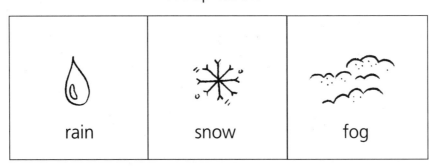

| rain | snow | fog |

Cloud Cover

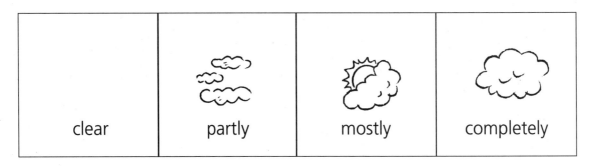

| clear | partly | mostly | completely |

Wind

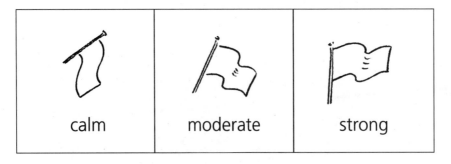

| calm | moderate | strong |

© Addison Wesley Publishing Company/Published by Dale Seymour Publications®

Environment Clip Art